WORLD EXPLORERS

FRANCISCO VÁSQUEZ DE CORONADO

An Explorer of the Southwest

by Amie Hazleton

CAPSTONE PRESS
a capstone imprint

Fact Finders Books are published by Capstone Press,
1710 Roe Crest Drive, North Mankato, Minnesota 56003
www.mycapstone.com

Library of Congress Cataloging-in-Publication Data
Names: Hazleton, Amie, author.
Title: Francisco Vásquez de Coronado : an explorer of the Southwest / by Amie
    Hazleton.
Description: North Mankato, Minnesota : Capstone Press, [2016] | Series: Fact
    finders. World explorers | Includes bibliographical references and index. |
    Audience: Ages 8–12.
Identifiers: LCCN 2016025970 | ISBN 9781515742036 (library binding) | ISBN
    9781515742074 (paperback) | ISBN 9781515742425 (eBook PDF)
Subjects: LCSH: Coronado, Francisco Vásquez de, 1510–1554—Juvenile literature.
    | Explorers — America—Biography—Juvenile literature. | Explorers—Spain—
    Biography—Juvenile literature. | Southwest, New—Description and travel—
    Juvenile literature. | America—Discovery and exploration—Spanish—Juvenile
    literature.
Classification: LCC E125.V3 H48 2016 | DDC 910.92 [B]—dc23
LC record available at https://lccn.loc.gov/2016025970

Editorial Credits:
Alesha Sullivan, editor; Kayla Rossow, designer; Wanda Winch, media researcher;
Laura Manthe, production specialist

Photo Credits:
Bridgeman Images: © Look and Learn/Private Collection/English School, 10, Peter
Newark American Pictures/Private Collection/Thomas Moran, 19, UIG/Universal
History Archive, 22; Capstone, 9; Courtesy of Richard G. Hogue studios, 20; Getty
Images: UIG/Universal History Archive, 13; National Geographic Creative: W.
Langdon Kihn, 17; NPS: Coronado National Memorial, 25, Coronado National
Memorial/Nevin Kempthorne, cover inset, 14, 27; Shutterstock: arigato, cardboard
texture, Dean Fikar, cover background, Ensuper, scratch paper texture, Nik Merkulov,
grunge paper element, run4it, watercolor paper element, Sunny Forest, sky design
element; SuperStock: SuperStock, 4

Printed in China.
009943S17

TABLE OF CONTENTS

Introduction

A Journey Begins

In the winter of 1540, a group of Spanish **nobles** gathered in New Spain, which is now known as Mexico. The men were about to embark on a journey led by Francisco Vásquez de Coronado. He hoped to find the rich cities of gold that were believed to lie to the north. Coronado's crew was one of the largest ever sent to explore the Americas. It was made up of more than 300 Spaniards and 1,000 native people. Herds of horses, cattle, pigs, and sheep were also brought along.

Coronado and his men in New Spain

Leading the **expedition**, Coronado sat on his finest horse. His golden armor glistened in the sunlight. As Coronado's soldiers rode past him, each man placed his hand on a prayer book and a cross. They swore to follow God, the king of Spain, and Coronado himself. Coronado's men happily took the oath. They believed that gold and glory was waiting for them up north, as Coronado promised. They expected to return to New Spain as rich men with stories to tell their families.

Coronado and his men would be gone for two years. They would travel more than 3,000 miles (4,828 kilometers) through the American southwest, claiming large regions of land for Spain. Coronado and his men would also be the first Europeans to explore the southern Great Plains, view the Grand Canyon, and live among the Pueblo Indians. Today Coronado's expedition is considered one of the most remarkable achievements in the history of exploration. But in Coronado's lifetime, it was seen as a total failure.

noble—aristocratic; belonging to a class with high social or political status

expedition—a long journey for a special purpose, such as exploring

Chapter 1

A MYSTERIOUS NEW WORLD

Many people believed that great riches of gold and treasure could be found north of New Spain. They had heard the legend of the Seven Cities of Cíbola told by native peoples in the area. According to the legend, the cities were filled with towering buildings that had walls of gold.

The first **viceroy** of New Spain, Antonio de Mendoza, had heard the legends of the cities of gold, but he believed they were myths. However, that changed in 1536 when a Spaniard named Álvar Núñez Cabeza de Vaca came to New Spain. Cabeza de Vaca was one of four men who had survived an expedition to Florida in 1527.

EXPLORING THE SOUTHWEST

Spain had controlled New Spain since 1521. That year, Spanish **conquistador** Hernán Cortés defeated the Aztec Indians. The Aztec's **empire** stretched across the region. Other Spaniards had already explored the lands south of New Spain, but no one had yet explored the vast area to the north.

For many years, Cabeza de Vaca lived with the native peoples. The natives told Cabeza de Vaca about large cities with tall buildings north of the New Spain region. The viceroy wondered if these could be the Seven Cities of Cíbola.

In 1539 Mendoza decided it was time to find out the truth about the cities. The viceroy sent a small crew to scout out the lands. Five months later the men returned with good news—the Seven Cities of Cíbola were real. Mendoza planned a larger expedition to the golden cities. He chose Coronado, a nobleman and close friend, to lead the exploration.

viceroy—a person sent by a king or queen to rule a colony
conquistador—a leader in the Spanish conquest of the Americas
empire—a group of countries that have the same ruler

Choosing a Leader

Francisco Vásquez de Coronado was born in Salamanca, Spain, in 1510. From a young age, Coronado seemed destined for fame. One of Coronado's friends even predicted that he would one day explore far-off lands. He envisioned that Coronado would hold a high position of power, but the final part of Coronado's life would not be happy. Coronado would suffer from a fall from which he would never recover.

Mendoza was named viceroy of New Spain in 1535. When he left his homeland for New Spain, he brought Coronado with him. A few short years later, Mendoza named Coronado the governor of New Galicia, a territory in northern New Spain. At the age of 30, Coronado was already a wealthy and important man. While governing New Galicia, Coronado proved himself to be a strong leader. He swiftly put down a slave uprising in his territory.

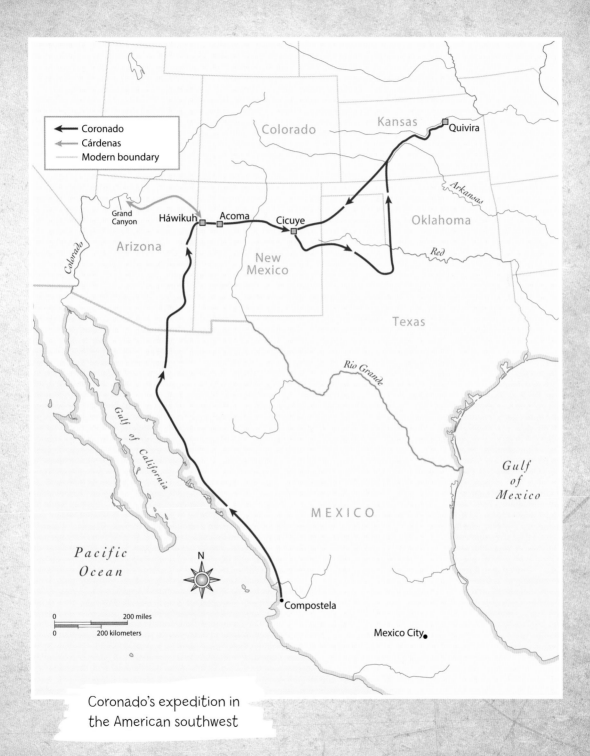

Coronado's expedition in the American southwest

Coronado led his men on a journey to find the gold rumored to be in the Seven Cities of Cíbola.

Coronado was also known throughout the region for doing good deeds. Mendoza believed that Coronado would treat the native people he encountered on his expedition with kindness, not cruelty. To ensure the trip was a success, Coronado brought along a Catholic priest named Fray Marcos de Niza. The priest, along with three other religious men, would talk to the natives about God and try and convert them to the Catholic religion.

But Fray Marcos joined the expedition for another reason—he had led Mendoza's earlier scouting trip to the north. He was the man who had seen the golden cities of Cíbola. "The city from where I beheld it looked splendid," he told the viceroy. "As well as I could judge, it is even larger than the city of Mexico." With Fray Marcos as a leader, Coronado believed he would soon have the riches from the Seven Cities of Cíbola in his hands.

Chapter 2

THE JOURNEY OF DEATH

Coronado and his men set off on February 23, 1540. But from the start, things went wrong. Fray Marcos had told Coronado that the roads were easy to travel over, but this was not true. The trails heading north were rough and dangerous. They had to cross mountains and deserts. They even had to cross over large rivers filled with alligators.

Coronado decided to send a scout ahead to see how the **terrain** looked. When the scout returned, he reported that he had seen hardly any silver or gold. The native people he spoke to said there were no majestic cities nearby. Coronado tried to keep the scout's information a secret, but word got out to his men.

Coronado and his men suffered harsh conditions traveling through the desert.

As summer neared, the weather and the rough journey started to take its toll. During the day the crew **sweltered** in the heat. But at night the men would have to huddle together for warmth. They suffered attacks from nearby native peoples, as well as snake bites and sickness caused by eating poisonous plants. Some of the crew died. As food and water became scarce, their spirits sank even lower. Some began calling the trip the "Journey of Death."

terrain—the surface of the land
swelter—to be uncomfortably hot

The Death of a Dream

On July 7, 1540, Coronado and his men arrived at the first city of Cíbola. Called Háwikuh, the city was a Zuni village with high stone walls. The Zuni people were native to this region. The city was located in present-day western New Mexico. Háwikuh was the city Fray Marcos claimed to have seen. But Háwikuh did not look the way Fray Marcos had described it.

Háwikuh

The city was not grand. It was a small, crowded village. Coronado's men were furious with Fray Marcos. As Coronado and his crew approached Háwikuh, some of the local villagers came outside. Coronado greeted them. He explained to the villagers that he had come to claim their village in the name of the king of Spain and of God. Coronado promised no harm, as long as they surrendered.

The Zuni people did nothing of the sort. They attacked Coronado and his men. Although Coronado did not want to fight the natives, he and his men needed to enter the village. They had traveled 1,500 miles (2,414 km), and they had no supplies left. Some of the men were dying of starvation. They needed food, so the Spaniards attacked the village.

FACT!

One of Coronado's men, Pedro de Castenada, called Háwikuh "a little crowded village ... all crumpled together."

Coronado, with his gold armor, was the main target of the villagers' stones and arrows. During the battle, Coronado was twice knocked from his horse by large stones. After the second fall, Coronado was pulled to safety by two of his men. "If I had not been protected by the very good **headpiece** which I wore, I think that the outcome would have been bad for me," Coronado told the viceroy.

The Spaniards were exhausted and hungry, but they managed to take over Háwikuh in only an hour. Inside the village Coronado and his men found corn, turkey, and beans. But they did not find any riches. To the Zuni people, Háwikuh was an important village and a center of trade for all nearby towns. Zuni people traded animal hides, shells, and turkey feathers—not gold, silver, and gemstones. The Seven Cities of Cíbola turned out to be a **fable**.

headpiece—a device worn on the head as an ornament or to serve a function

fable—a made-up story that isn't true

The Spanish conquistadors quickly took over the village of Háwikuh.

Fray Marcos feared for his safety. He headed back to New Spain. Coronado sent a letter to the viceroy saying, "I can assure you that in reality Fray Marcos has not told the truth in a single thing he said. The Seven Cities are seven little villages." Coronado told his friend that the only treasure he had found so far were some stone crystals and pieces of emerald, a green gemstone.

Chapter 3

A GLIMMER OF HOPE

Coronado was disappointed, but he wanted to make the most of his trip. He insisted on finding out if the surrounding regions held anything worthwhile, such as gold. Coronado sent out four scouting parties to survey the area. One group was told to search the nearby villages of the Hopi people. A second group was sent west to meet up with Spanish supply ships sent from New Spain. Neither group was successful.

FACT!

The Pueblo Indian village of Acoma is known as the "sky city" because it sits on top of a huge rock rising high above the plains.

A third group, led by García López de Cárdenas, was instructed to find the "great river" to the west. Cárdenas and his crew journeyed to the south rim of the Grand Canyon, becoming the first Europeans to view this natural wonder. Although the men looked for a way to reach the bottom of the canyon, they could not find one.

Hernando de Alvarado led the fourth group. He and 20 men were sent to explore the land to the east of New Spain. Throughout his trip Alvarado was greeted warmly by the people he met. One village he visited was the Pueblo town of Acoma. During their explorations, Alvarado and his men became the first Europeans to describe the huge herds of buffalo that freely roamed the plains.

Acoma

Alvarado continued traveling through the plains. At a village called Cicuye, he met a Native American who was nicknamed "the Turk." The Turk had an exciting story to tell. Not only had he heard of the seven golden cities, he knew exactly where they were. They could be found in the Turk's homeland—a place called Quivira.

Coronado and his men headed for Quivira in the hope of discovering gold.

The Turk spun several stories for Alvarado and his men. He said the chief of the kingdom had a boat with a large golden eagle on the front. Each afternoon the chief napped under a tree with small gold bells hanging from it. The bells put him to sleep as they chimed in the air. The Turk claimed that gold was so common in Quivira that everyone ate from plates made of gold.

When Coronado caught wind of the Turk's stories, he was thrilled. Coronado wanted to head east to Quivira when spring arrived. On April 23, 1541, Coronado, his men, and the Turk left the winter camp in search of the riches of Quivira. They may have traveled along the Arkansas River, following what is now the modern-day Santa Fe Trail. The men **trekked** all summer long, passing through Texas, Oklahoma, and into the center of what is now Kansas. The farther Coronado went, the more discouraged he became. Coronado was convinced that the Turk was lying to him about the gold.

trek—to make a slow, difficult journey

When the group reached Quivira, they found just another Native American village, home to the Wichita people. Their homes were cone-shaped huts with straw roofs. Crops filled the nearby fields. Although Coronado found pumpkins, corn, and tobacco, he found no gold.

a Wichita lodge

The Turk had fooled them. He admitted that he had been lying. He told Coronado that he had intended to lead him and his men into the wilderness and abandon them. The Turk had hopes that Coronado would not be able to find his way home and would die in the wild. Coronado had the Turk executed.

THE TURK

The Turk played an important part in Coronado's expedition. While in Cicuye the Spaniards became acquainted with the Turk, who was a Native American slave. He was from the region east of the Mississippi River. He told the Spaniards many stories, including the Quivira gold story that led Coronado east. The Turk enhanced his story by telling Coronado he possessed many gold bracelets, but that the bracelets were taken from him when he was captured. Coronado believed the Turk and asked Alvarado to retrieve the Turk's gold bracelets in Cicuye. The people of Cicuye knew nothing of the gold bracelets, but Coronado refused to believe the truth. The Spaniards took an elder native captive in chains for the bracelets when the men left for Quivira.

Chapter 4

RETURN TO NEW SPAIN

Coronado left Quivira and headed back to their camp in New Spain. His hopes were destroyed. In a letter to the king of Spain, Coronado wrote of Quivira: "And what I am sure of is that there is not any gold nor any other metal in all that country." Coronado also told the king that he did not feel that Spain should establish any settlements in the land to the north.

FACT!

Father Juan de Padilla, a priest who traveled to Kansas with Coronado, returned to the Wichita village to preach one year after Coronado's trip. Shortly after, he was killed by natives.

During the journey south, Coronado fell off his horse and was severely injured. When he recovered, he wanted to continue home to New Spain. Two months later, Coronado and 100 of his men finally made it back home. The rest of the crew straggled in later—tired, poor, and unhappy.

While only a few of Coronado's men made the return to New Mexico, the expedition began with over 1,000 soldiers, Indian allies and slaves, as well as livestock and supplies.

Most people in Spain and New Spain considered Coronado's expedition a failure. Two years later, the explorer was brought to trial. He was accused of **mismanaging** the trip and treating many native people cruelly. Coronado was not found guilty of any of the charges. One of his conquistadors, however, was convicted of cruelty to native people.

On September 22, 1554, Coronado died in Mexico City at the age of 44. He never understood how important his expedition was. Several decades later the Spanish would establish settlements in the lands Coronado explored. These were some of the first European settlements in what would later become the United States.

Much later, huge quantities of silver, copper, and other valuable metals would be found in the American southwest. The region did in fact hold great riches, if not the ones sought by Coronado. They were there for the taking—just beneath the ground.

mismanage—to handle badly

Francisco Vásquez de Coronado

Timeline

1510: Francisco Vásquez de Coronado is born in Salamanca, Spain

1521: Hernán Cortés conquers the Aztec Indians

1535: Antonio de Mendoza is named the viceroy of New Spain

1536: Álvar Núñez Cabeza de Vaca arrives in New Spain, telling tales of large cities with tall buildings

1539: Viceroy Mendoza sends a small party of explorers to scout the land to the north of New Spain

February 1540: Coronado and his expedition begin their search for the Seven Cities of Cíbola

July 1540: the Zuni village of Háwikuh is taken over by Coronado and his men

1541: Coronado and his men journey east to Quivira, where there is rumored to be gold

1542: Coronado returns to New Spain

1554: Coronado dies in Mexico City

Important People

Hernando de Alvarado (?)—led a group of men from Coronado's expedition who became the first Europeans to see the High Plains region of the United States

Álvar Núñez Cabeza de Vaca (c. 1490–1560)—Spanish explorer; member of 1527 expedition to Florida who lived among the native peoples for several years before his return to New Spain in 1536

Pedro de Castenada (?)—member of Coronado's crew who later wrote an account of the expedition

Hernán Cortés (1485–1547)—conqueror of Mexico's Aztec Empire

García López de Cárdenas (?)—Spanish explorer; member of Coronado's expedition who led the group of first Europeans to see the Grand Canyon

Antonio de Mendoza (c. 1490–1552)—first viceroy of New Spain; he put Coronado in charge of the expedition in search of the Seven Cities of Cíbola

Fray (Friar) Marcos de Niza (c. 1495–1558)—missionary and explorer who claimed to have seen one of the Seven Cities of Cíbola

"The Turk" (?)—Native American who told Coronado that the Seven Cities were in his homeland of Quivira

GLOSSARY

conquistador (kon-KEYS-tuh-dor)—a leader in the Spanish conquest of the Americas

empire (EM-pire)—a group of countries that have the same ruler

expedition (ek-spuh-DISH-uhn)—a long journey for a special purpose, such as exploring

fable (FAY-buhl)—a made-up story that isn't true

headpiece (HED-peess)—a device worn on the head as an ornament or to serve a function

mismanage (MISS-man-ij)—to handle badly

noble (NOH-buhl)—aristocratic; belonging to a class with high social or political status

swelter (SWEL-tuhr)—to be uncomfortably hot

terrain (tuh-RAYN)—the surface of the land

trek (TREK)—to make a slow, difficult journey

viceroy (VICE-roi)—a person sent by a king or queen to rule a colony

READ MORE

Cooke, Tim. *Explore with Francisco Vasquez de Coronado.* Travel with the Great Explorers. New York: Crabtree Publishing, 2016.

Kallen, Stuart, A. *A Journey with Francisco Coronado. Primary Source Explorers.* Minneapolis, Minn.: Lerner Publications, 2017.

McDaniel, Melissa. *Southwest Indians. First Nations of North America.* Chicago: Heinemann Library, 2012.

INTERNET SITES

FactHound offers a safe, fun way to find Internet sites related to this book. All of the sites on FactHound have been researched by our staff.

Here's all you do:

Visit *www.facthound.com*

Type in this code: 9781515742036

Check out projects, games and lots more at
www.capstonekids.com

CRITICAL THINKING USING THE COMMON CORE

1. Why did Antonio de Mendoza choose Coronado to lead an expedition in the American southwest in 1539? (Key Ideas and Details)

2. Why do you think the Turk misled Coronado and his men by telling fables of the golden cities? (Integration of Knowledge and Ideas)

3. Do you think Coronado's expedition was a success or failure? Why? (Integration of Knowledge and Ideas)

INDEX